WISDOM WISE

Marilyn Edwards

Kingdom Publishers

WISDOM WISE
Copyright© Marilyn Edwards

All rights reserved. No part of this book may be reproduced in any form by photocopying or any electronic or mechanical means, including information storage or retrieval systems, without permission in writing from both the copyright owner and the publisher of the book. The right of Marilyn Edwards to be identified as the author of this work has been asserted by him/her in accordance with the Copyright, Designs and Patents Act 1988 and any subsequent amendments thereto.
A catalogue record for this book is available from the British Library.

ISBN: 978-1-913247-19-5

1st Edition by Kingdom Publishers
Kingdom Publishers
London, UK.

You can purchase copies of this book from any leading bookstore or email
contact@kingdompublishers.co.uk

Abba Father I thank you for your prompting, inspiration and the ability to write that which is laid on my heart. I dedicate this book to the people who are special to me.

Proverbs 4:7: "Wisdom is the principal thing, therefore get wisdom and with all our getting get understanding".

CONTENT

CHAPTER ONE
    Why did the Heathen Rage   9
    Condemned to Die   11
    Freedom   12
    Risen King   13

CHAPTER TWO
    Jehovah God Sees   14
    Return to Me   15
    God's Will   16
    Unity   17

CHAPTER THREE
    Where Are You Lord   18
    Hide Me Lord   19

CHAPTER FOUR
    First Fruit   20

CHAPTER FIVE
    Dispose   22
    Shadow   23
    Jehovah God I Come   24
    Next Level   25
    Don't Judge Christ by me   26
    God's Tabernacle   27

CHAPTER SIX
    I Hurt like You   28
    What's that I hear   29
    Testimonies   30

CHAPTER SEVEN
    Shh!   31
    I Hear Riot   32
    It's Loud   34
    Stand Strong   36

CHAPTER EIGHT
    God's Word   37
    Worship   38

CHAPTER NINE
    Listen   39
    Atmospheric Posture   40
    The Sun   42

CHAPTER TEN
    I Wisdom   43
    Calling Wisdom   44
    Wisdom Speaks   45
    Wisdom Wise   46
    Wisdom Cries Here I Am   47

CHAPTER ONE

WHY DID THE HEATHEN RAGE

Why did the Heathen rage
And the people plot a vain thing
They came together to take counsel
To destroy the King.

In their hearts they had no fear
They spoke lies and accusations but did not care
Some looked on with disbelief
Others cheered as their eyes filled with glee.

Wickedness aroused in their heart
Indicating their hated
Who knew Jesus was the Saviour
Turned their backs
Those who were unsure the enemy played havoc.

Christ future through Jehovah God was vindicated
No house had He vacated
For the Son of man had nowhere to lay His head
Stone craving and on soft ground was where He made His bed.

All saw Him as the Shepherd's Son
How could He possibly be the redeeming one
The law they knew but could not tell
As they read the scrolls that made them swell.

Some shouted out He is the Christ
But others gathered for Him to be crucified
Though the scriptures had to be fulfilled
It was a cold and callous way to kill the King.

His body was beaten with cat-o-nine tail
Tearing His skin that hid the veil
What a price to pay for mankind
His kingdom forever reigns as His glory shines.

CONDEMNED TO DIE

Jesus was arrested and condemned to die
By His own who knew not why
They hated him and wanted to make a show
Of the one who called himself King.

They thought it was great
So they laughed at Him
When the thorns was placed on His head
They jeered and squealed while they wished Him dead.

As Jesus walked along
Weighed down by the Cross He dragged
None of the faces who jeered at Him looked sad
Their faces were masked with pride
As the pleasure in their heart they did not hide.

Jesus would look as He struggled on by
With the cross He carried on which He would die
Through drops of blood
His eyes saw hate
In the eyes of those who did not see His fate as a mistake.

FREEDOM

Abba Father
You gave your Son Jesus Christ
Whose blood was shed to set us free
You used His life to give us a chance
To repent of our sins and receive liberty.

When you gave your only Begotten Son
You knew the battle had been won
You gave so all could heal
And man could change his heart of steel.

Through Him you healed the lame
He did miracles that were not the same
You sent many Prophets ahead of Him
So that the way would be made to caste away our sins.

Even though you knew He would be met with unbelief
It pleased You to shed His blood for man's relief.

RISEN KING

Jesus Christ the risen King
Oh to you I cling
For salvation to the nation you bring
That no man would be lost
As you purchased them at a cost.

Your blood was split on Calvary Hill
Every action seen appeared against your will
Shouts were heard from voices
Who cried, crucify Him.

Three days later the Resurrected One
Showed himself as He appeared to His fellow men
He reminded them of why He was sent.

Some of the disciples believed, Thomas doubted
But upon seeing His nail pierced hands was totally relieved
Jesus turn to him and said
Blessed are those who have not seen but yet believe.

CHAPTER TWO

JEHOVAH GOD SEES

If you could see what I see
You would know what I think of thee
Your inner man is what I plan
To change and make like me.

Hide not yourself away
For you the debt I paid
To see the light I placed inside
To make you walk my way.

RETURN TO ME

Return to me say the Lord
Your sins I will pardon
And your obedience I will reward.

Come let us reason together
Though your sins be as scarlet
I'll make them white as snow
Though they be red like crimson
They shall be as wool.

Once you are forgiven
There is no need for you to make others
Place your mind back in prison.

GOD'S WILL

When the opposite sex say they love you check it out
Check it out with the Lord before you shout
Is it God's plan or is it yours
Don't forget it must line up with His word.

Remember your flesh is not skilled
Satan will send counterfeit to entice your will
He will send those to distract
So please, please tell him to get back.

With the flesh there are feelings
With the Holy Spirit wisdom and reasoning
Many times we think we are flowing
But sometimes it is because of our pass knowing.

UNITY

Lord teach us as a Church to unite
To humble ourselves and not to fuss and fight
To treat our men like brothers
And our women like sisters
The older women like spiritual mothers
The aged men as wisdom givers
To be truthful in what we do
Kind and gentle too.

CHAPTER THREE

WHERE ARE YOU LORD

Lord, where are you when I call
I look for you down the hall
But I cannot see a thing
Because it's black and bleak within.

Why are you not there?
Why can't I see?
Why is Satan playing tricks on me?
I hold my breath as I listen
All I can hear is my heartbeat quicken.

I sense you now
Your presence feels warm
Oh my Lord now I recall
How when you are near
There is a difference in the air.

My hands feels tingly
My eyes are clear as I stare
I see bright lights just over there
Thank you Lord for you truly care.

HIDE ME LORD

To you Lord I lift my hands
And give you all the praise
The glory that shines from above
Received through your eternal love.

Hide me in the shadow of your wings
From the wicked who assays
Pull that chain that tries to keep me bound
From around me I pray.

Place your edge of protection
Mercy and love in that same place.

CHAPTER FOUR

FIRST FRUIT

I was going through a test
Feeling hurt, confused and vexed
While I went through things in my head
I felt weak, I felt dread.

I sought the Holy Spirit
I asked what I can hear
This test must be a way to draw me near.

I promised the Lord I would draw close
Give up things to fulfil this post
Only the Lord can look deep inside
Turning it outside so that I cannot hide.

Wanting me to hear and see
Guess what the Holy Spirit said to me
Honour the Lord with the first fruit of your substance
I did not catch it at first
I said, "Lord I do this anyway
Every week I give and sometimes more".

Hey this is correct but guess what came next
Honour the Lord with your sacrifice of praise
Worship, studying time and meditation of my Word
But don't do it in haste.

I realised that even though I did these things
Sometimes there were distractions within
My mind would wonder
My hands would move
But it was not a substance the Lord required to use.

Help me Lord I asked
Let me do your will
Have you way
And make me be still.

CHAPTER FIVE

DISPOSE

A smile, a weep, a teardrop fall
As all inside is shared with all
No secrets no longer there to keep
No memories to hide away sins seep

SHADOW

Why should I be a shadow you see
Wanting, seeking forever in large degree
Why when I speak you do not hear
Hearts apart just wanting to share.

Needs amiss, what's this
Only to succeed in what you think it fits
Time will tell, oh, oh well
In the end what it spells.

JEHOVAH GOD I COME

Naked I came and naked you took
Not a second glance or a curious look
I came undress so you could see
The true, real and faulty me.

As I stood in your presence
I could feel your Holy reverence
Your sweet perfume was the scent
Your holiness I comprehend.

You stripped me further
My inner coat which I could not see
You cleansed and delivered me
From all uncleanness in my body.

You dressed me with the very best
Jesus Christ holiness
His richness, glory and strength
And this I clothe myself with until eternity ends.

NEXT LEVEL

Can you see your destiny?
Is it clear before you?
The promises God has given
Laid up for you in heaven.

He has opened the door so wide
But travelling along you realise
The cross you bare seems to want to tare
Those promises He gave.

Your torn between the now and then
As the problems increase and becomes intense
Your eyes stare through the little view
That is left inside of you.

Write the vision it will not tarry
Your cross you need to bare
What you will see in the end
Are the fruits that comes through all the cares.

DON'T JUDGE CHRIST BY ME

Don't judge Christ by me
I'm only a speck, maybe a branch fallen off the tree
He's given me the means to bear fruit
If this does not come forth
It's not Him that caused me not to produce.

He has given me instructions to live by
I can either use them or say bye, bye
If what you have seen does not show who He is
Don't shy away and say He's not real, just call on Him.

He did not say we would be perfect
Neither did He say we would not make mistakes
But He did say when these things happen
Remember He Jesus who lives in you is great.

GOD'S TABENACLE

You are the house that God built
He did not make you messed up as you think
Sin came through Adam and with one blink
All that God promised became like it drained down the sink.

You are His tabernacle where His spirit dwells
When it is filled things will work out well
As we rely on the Holy Spirit and His wisdom
His precepts and statues will draw us into the Kingdom.

CHAPTER SIX

I HURT LIKE YOU

You're not the only one who hurts
God has made everyone from dirt
Why is it so hard to see
I'm like you and you're like me.

My pain may not be yours
And your pain may not be mine
But hurt is still to me and you so unkind.

When you're in pain
Don't tell me I do not understand
I've gone through just like you
With the strength of Jehovah God is how I came through.

WHAT'S THAT I HEAR?

My mind was vex
It gets complex
I want my needs
It must be met
Holding, coping no more joking
Trials they come, sometimes in sum
Unable to be multiplied.

What's that I hear
A flicker of tear
It drops, need strength to make it stop
I hear a voice,
Holy Spirit tell me I have a choice.

Why is your soul caste down
When the Word I speak is your crown
Weeping may endure for a night
But joy comes in the morning light.

Peace, peace awake
Joy, joy it's no mistake.

TESTIMONIES

I was about to go to sleep
But suddenly I felt wide awake
I reflected on the day and what I heard
Testimonies of your goodness
Bible scriptures and verse
All pronouncing the beauty of an awesome God
Who always keep His Word.

The day was filled with meaning
And a need to look within
As others were really open
To painful and precious things.

Pass hurts and struggles
Which they have now overcome
It was awesome to hear
The things that the Redeemer had done
And to see the faces of others as hope suddenly sprung.

CHAPTER SEVEN

SHH!

Shh to the voices that I can hear around me and inside my head
Shh to those voices that sound loud and louder than my mind instead
Shh I say because the Word of God tells me
My sheep hear my voice and no stranger do they follow.

Shh you who want to come louder and louder
I silence you in the name of Jesus Christ of Nazareth
I am His sheep, I am His sheep
Called from darkness to light
I am His sheep reconciled
Set free and now at His right side.

Shh to those voices so that I can hear
The still small voice of the one who truly cares
My Redeemer, my Saviour, my love and my all
Shh to those voices I will not recall.

I HEAR RIOT

Listen can you hear the riot
It thunders behind
It thunders before
It thunders on the right
It thunders on the left.

Can you hear the riot
The things that's thrown at you
You seek for peace to pursue
But the riot, the noise is so loud.

You sit and you cover your ears to block out
And inside your heart you shout
Quiet, quiet, quiet
Be still, STOP!

You remove your hands from your ears
But still the riot
You look to your left
You look to your right

But there's nothing in sight
You sit still and you realise that the riot is within.

Can you hear the riot?
You stare because you realise that you need to share
You need to share with the Saviour all the things that's there
You open your mouth and you look up
You shout, Jesus, Jesus please make it stop
Take me out of this noise
Take me out of this riot.

You hear Him now because you are ready to declare
You hear a still small voice
Open your heart and let Him in
For peace through Jesus the Holy Spirit will bring.

You suddenly feel a relief
The things inside you were such heap
You smile for awhile
And you say Jesus I am your child.

IT'S LOUD

Drown out the noise
I don't want to think
If I could just fill my mind with things
Yes, go on the phone and use that link.

Drown out the noise it's too intense
I know what I'll do I'll call on a friend
Speak for hours so there's talk in my ears
It will lessen my cares.

Drown out that noise when I'm alone
Turn up the music volume on the microphone
Then I won't hear those voices anymore
Or maybe they will just lessen for sure.

In the end does it really go
Or does reality surface and show
After the call and the music has gone
The noise returns with a BIG BANG.

Fill your mind with what will bring life
The Word of God that so many criticise
As its entrance is like new wine
Rich, embodied and refined.

STAND STRONG

Stand strong, stand strong
For He is God and you are man
Stand strong, stand strong
His face to seek
His Word to speak.

Let the redeem shout I am strong
For God delivered you from the destroyers plan
Stand strong, stand strong.

Stand up and hold your head up high
He has already done it so don't you cry
Just stand strong, stand strong
You are in the Father's plan.

CHAPTER EIGHT

GOD'S WORD

The Word of God brings light
To help us to see things right
It's like a lamp unto our feet
If we walk in it, it will esteem.

WORSHIP

Worship is an inner connection of our Soul with Father God
An expression of what He gives us freely.
Worship is unquestionable and undeniable
An inner substance enhanced by knowing God's Word.
The essence of His deity
The flavour and substance of who we are to be.

It's an expression that will not deny
The embodiment of who we are in Jesus eyes
The crevice of our totality
As we worship Him in full degree
Praises, prayer, adoration, exaltation, studying and loving is His Divinity.

To worship in spirit and in truth is what He Yahweh God requires
So let us line up with His desires.

CHAPTER NINE

LISTEN

A quiet and still morning speech
Looking at the clouds in the sky
Some are large and some are small
Touching heaven firmament and all.

It's hard to understand as the clouds are formed
Waters, vapours coming tall
A tear to compare
As the sea rustles forward but still looks bare
The wind blowing everything until suddenly there is nothing there.

Storming billows rolls and rolls
Crying tears from coast to coast
Going high as a mountain top
Holding on to what cannot stop

Peace, peace as the waters run down
Forming patterns of joy and hope
Silence is felt all around
As tears, raindrops and billows fold
Caressing as they come together in their final hold.

ATMOSPERIC POSTURE

Intensified in what is wrong
Looking for the strong
Weakness explodes, a long way to go
Heaven looks, clouds flow
The sky is blue, the sea shows.

What can it be but a mist along
Blowing the weak to make them strong
The wild berries that looks like buttons
The weak may look but only see cotton.

They may weep a tear or two
In their strength they may be few
It's down to hope for all to know
It is only time that unfolds.

Its thoughts no one can tell
The earth continues in its shell
Why sky, why moon, why stars that looms
Why earth and galaxies consumed.

A big wide world that holds its own
The wonders of creation shown

Men given dominion over the things that's real
Fallen but now risen up with Christ redeemed.

THE SUN

The sun shines hot
It's like a dot
In the firmament of the sky
Uniquely placed so that no man can questions why.

It beams its rays
Through the days
At night it quietly goes
Out comes the moon
And the stars and the light to expose.

The glory of the Father who created them all
The magnitude of how they are seen we will always recall.

CHAPTER TEN

I WISDOM

Wisdom cries out
Incline your ears to me
When wisdom enters your heart
She will never displease.

CALLING WISDOM

I emptied myself of all I had
So you Lord could strip away what's bad
You took your hands and held me up as everything I gave
So not to allow the battle within to have its way.

I cried Wisdom where were you when I was not standing tall
Did I shut you out because on you I did not want to call
Fill me deep within
As all the places that's empty now, I allow you in.

I put you as a crown on my head
And bind you around my neck
I now rely on you Wisdom to guide me through every test.

WISDOM SPEAKS

Wisdom speaks
Can you hear
Just listen and be still
She cries to your mind
She cries to your heart
She cries to your will.

WISDOM WISE

The fear of the Lord is the beginning of wisdom
Did you hear what I said?
Fools despise it and instructions
That's because they are spiritually dead.

Wisdom from God above is pure
We all need it that's for sure
When we find it we'll get understanding
As Wisdom is always knocking at the door.

She is more precious than silver
More valuable than gold
Her value is truly untold
Do not forsake her and she will keep you
When you walk down the road she will be there to meet you.

WISDOM CRIES HERE I AM

Wisdom cries, here I am
With a big mighty shout
Take me into your bosom
And speak of me with your mouth.

Happy is the man that finds me
To him I will bring honour and grace
When he embrace and take me into his space.

I Wisdom am more precious than rubies
Please don't turn away and refuse me
Length of days are in my hands
I Wisdom was not created by man.

By me Wisdom the earth was found
Through understanding the heaven abound
And by knowledge the depths are broken
And the clouds drops down their drew
Therefore keep sound wisdom for she is pleasant
She will elevate you.

www.ingramcontent.com/pod-product-compliance
Lightning Source LLC
Chambersburg PA
CBHW071039080526
44587CB00015B/2686